Dolphins

Patricia Kendell

An imprint of ...en's Books

in the wild

Chimpanzees Dolphins Elephants
Lions Polar Bears Tigers

© 2002 White-Thomson Publishing Ltd

Produced for Hodder Wayland by White-Thomson Publishing Ltd

Editor: Kay Barnham
Designer: Tim Mayer
Picture research: Shelley Noronha – Glass Onion Pictures
Consultant: Dr Sian Pullen is the Head of WWF's Marine and
   Coastal Policy team.
Language Consultant: Norah Granger, Senior Lecturer in Primary
   Education at the University of Brighton.

Published in Great Britain in 2002 by Hodder Wayland,
an imprint of Hodder Children's Books
This paperback edition published in 2002
Reprinted in 2003
The right of Patricia Kendell to be identified as the author of this
Work has been asserted by her in accordance with the Copyright,
Designs and Patents Act 1988.

Photograph acknowledgements:
Bruce Coleman 3 (second), 21 (Charles & Sandra Hood),
4 (Jorg & Petra Wegner), 5, 6 (Franco Banfi), 10 (Jeff Foott),
16 (James D Watt/Watt Wildlife Library), 17; Ecoscene 24
(Quentin Bares); FLPA 3 (fourth), 13 (K Webber/Earthviews),
8 (L Sorisio/Panda), 9 (Minden Pictures), 18 (D P Wilson),
27 (F Nicklin), 29 (Derek Hall); Michael Holford 20;
NHPA 7, 23 (A N T), 18 & 19 (Norbert Wu); Oxford Scientific
Films 1, 3 (third), 15 (Clive Bromhall), 12, 32 (Gerard Soury);
Still Pictures 3 (first), 11 (Horst Schafer), 14 (Robert Henno),
22 (Jeffrey Rotman), 25 (S Dawson), 26 (David Woodfall),
28 (Mark Cawardine).

British Library Cataloguing in Publication Data
Kendell, Patricia
 Dolphins. - (In the wild)
 1. Dolphins I. Title
 599.5'3

 ISBN: 0 7502 4000 8

Printed in Hong Kong by Wing King Tong Co. Ltd

Hodder Children's Books
A division of Hodder Headline
338 Euston Road, London NW1 3BH

Produced in association with WWF-UK.
WWF-UK registered charity number 1081247.
A company limited by guarantee number 4016725.
Panda device © 1986 WWF ® WWF registered trademark owner.

Contents

Where dolphins live

Dolphins are **mammals**. They live in seas and rivers all over the world. These are bottlenose dolphins. You can see them in the seas around Britain.

Dolphins are close **relatives** of whales and porpoises.
There are over 40 different kinds of dolphin.
The orca is one of the largest.

5

Baby dolphins

A baby dolphin is called a calf. As soon as it is born,
its mother takes it to the **surface** to breathe air.
Dolphins need to breathe to survive.

A dolphin breathes air through a **blowhole** on top of its head. Its sleek, streamlined body is ideal for swimming.

Looking after the calves

The mother dolphin squirts milk into the calf's mouth. The milk is very creamy. It gives the calf energy to grow quickly.

Each calf stays close to its mother, so that she can protect it from danger.

Growing up

Dolphins keep in touch with their young as they grow older. A mother calls to her calves with a special whistle that they will recognise all their lives.

Young dolphins learn how to make friends.

Family life

Dolphins live and work in a group called a school.

They often play together.
These dolphins are having fun!

Rest and play

A dolphin cannot fall deeply asleep underwater. It would drown. Instead it stays half asleep for part of the day.

This dolphin is enjoying surfing on the waves.

Communicating

These Atlantic spotted dolphins are finding their way around by sending sounds through the water. When a sound hits something, it bounces back to the dolphin as an **echo**.

Sometimes, loud noises made at
sea by drilling for oil can confuse
dolphins. They find it hard to send
and receive messages.

Hunting

Dolphins eat **squid** and
fish like these grey mullet.

Sometimes, dolphins **herd** fish
to make them easier to catch.

Dolphins and people

People have always been fascinated by stories about dolphins. This **mosaic** was made by Romans about 2,000 years ago.

Today people enjoy swimming in the sea with these clever, friendly animals.

Keeping safe

Dolphins have to watch out for sharks,
which may attack them.

They protect themselves with their many teeth, sometimes using their beaks as battering rams.

Threats

People can catch lots of fish in huge nets, leaving fewer fish for dolphins to eat.

Sometimes, dolphins get caught in fishing nets.
They cannot go up for air and so they drown.

Dolphins in danger

When **dangerous chemicals** get into the sea, they can poison the food that dolphins eat.

Building **dams** on rivers and draining lakes
leaves fewer places where creatures like this
Brazilian dolphin can live.

Helping dolphins to survive

We need to find out much more about dolphins and make **laws** to protect them properly.

Places must be found where dolphins and whales can live safely, like this dolphin **sanctuary** in Australia.

Further information

Find out more about how we can help dolphins in the future.

ORGANISATIONS TO CONTACT

WWF-UK
Panda House, Weyside Park,
Godalming, Surrey GU7 1XR
Tel: 01483 426444
http://www.wwf-uk.org

Whale and Dolphin Conservation Society
Brookfield House, 38 St Paul Street,
Chippenham, Wiltshire SN15 1LY
Tel: 01249 449500

The Wildlife Trust, Cornwall
Five Acres, Allet, Truro,
Cornwall TR4 9DJ
Tel: 01872 273939
http://www.cornwallwildlifetrust.org.uk

Sea Watch Foundation
36 Windmill Road, Headington
Oxford OX3 7BX
Tel: 01865 764794
http://www.seawatchfoundation.org.uk

BOOKS

Our Wild World: Dolphins: Julia Vogel &
John F. McGee, Northword 2001.

Is a Dolphin a Fish?: Melvin Berger, Gilda
Berger & Karen Carr, Scholastic Reference
2002.

Dolphins: Claire Robinson, Heinemann
2000.

**A Visual Introduction to Whales, Dolphins
and Porpoises:** Martin Camm (Animal
Watch series), Cherry Tree Books 2002.

WEBSITES

Most young children will need adult help
when visiting websites. Those listed have
child-friendly pages that could be
bookmarked.

www.panda.org/kids/wildlife
Includes a dolphin and porpoises quiz.

http://www.whaleclub.com/
The Whale Club's website, with facts, advice and stories from young dolphin watchers.

http://www.seaweb.org
All the latest news from Seaweb.

http://www.mcsuk.org
Facts and photographs from the Marine Conservation Society. Includes information on how to get involved with conservation.

http://www.wdcs.org
The Whale and Dolphin Conservation Society campaigns to protect whales and dolphins around the world.

Visit learn.co.uk for more resources

Glossary

blowhole – where dolphins breathe in and out at the surface of the water.

dam – a barrier across a river to hold the water in a big pool.

dangerous chemicals – chemicals that harm the environment.

echo – a sound that bounces back so it is heard again.

herd – to move in a large group.

laws – rules that people must follow.

mammals – warm-blooded animals. Females produce milk to feed their young.

mosaic – a picture or pattern made with small pieces of coloured stone or glass.

relatives – members of the same family.

sanctuary – a safe place.

squid – sea creatures with ten tentacles.

surface – the top of something, in this case the sea.

Index